The Adventures of the Pirate
The Dragons Treasure

Authors: David Powell & Krista Tarasyuk Watkins.

Illustrations: David Powell, fiverr & Istock.

Contributors: fiverr, Pixabay and Brusheazy

Donations: Spiritwolf-Photography.com

Permissions: Special Thanks to
Lisa   The Mousehole, Quay St
           Mousehole.
              Cornwall
              England.

For giving a fitting home to the Pirate Mice.

Teddy Bear

Captain Cheddar.

Stilton.

Pam Ezan.

Gordon Zola.

Wensley Dale.

Matilda

Sid

Mrs Mouse and family.

Wyvern

Daisy Dolphin.

It was a hot summer's day,
The pirate mice sailed The Leaky Bucket into the bay.
They docked in the safe harbour of Cornwall.
The village of Mousehole has it all.

The mice are so happy to finally be home.
Their adventure was great but they felt so alone.
Pam Ezan spotted the gift shop, her family's house.
Thinking "Mousehole, is the best place to live, for a mouse.'

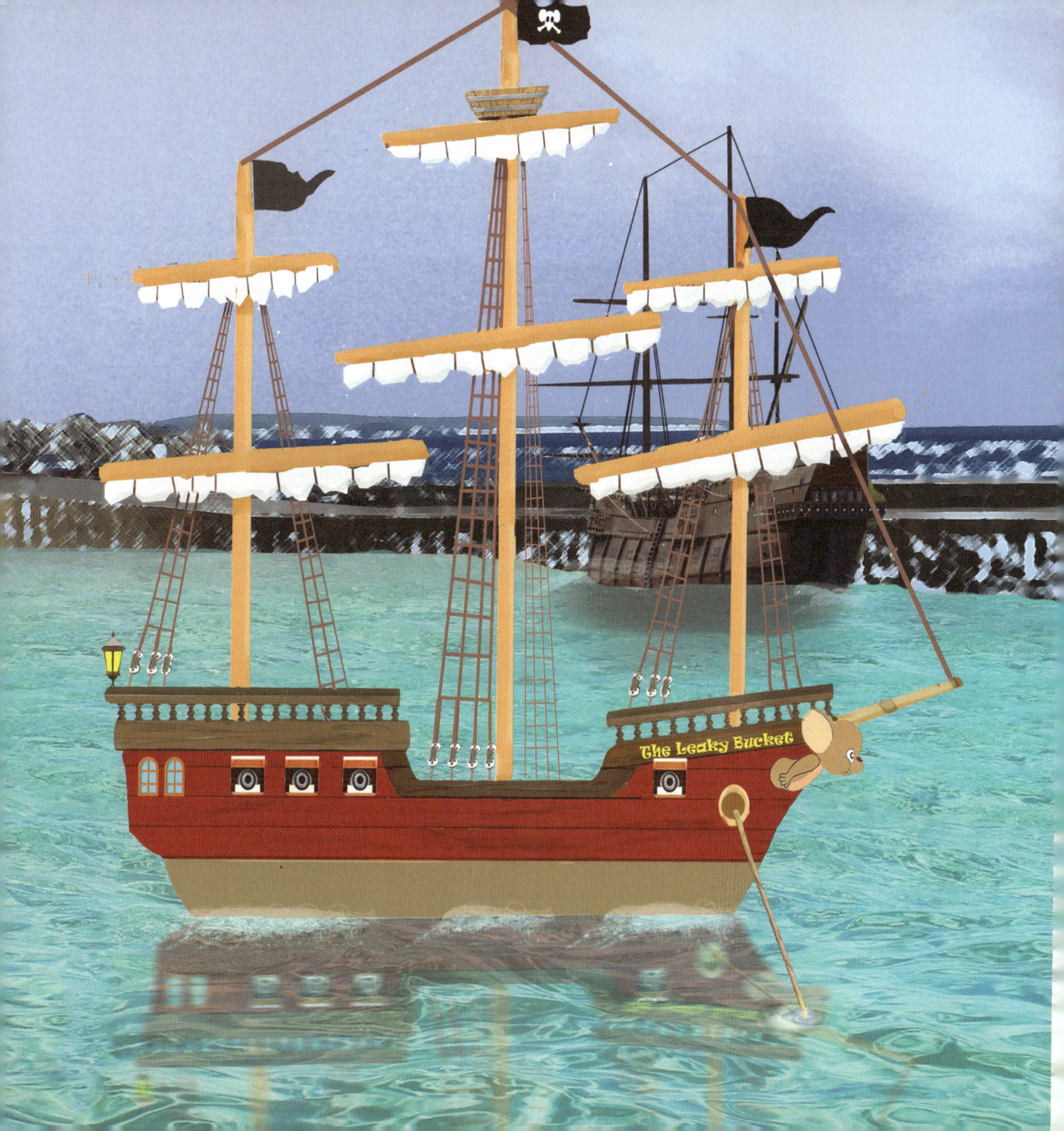
The Leaky Bucket

Captain Cheddar and Pam left the ship in a tick. They had been feeling so very home sick. While they are walking they saw two young mice, dressed in ragged clothes with nautical stripes.

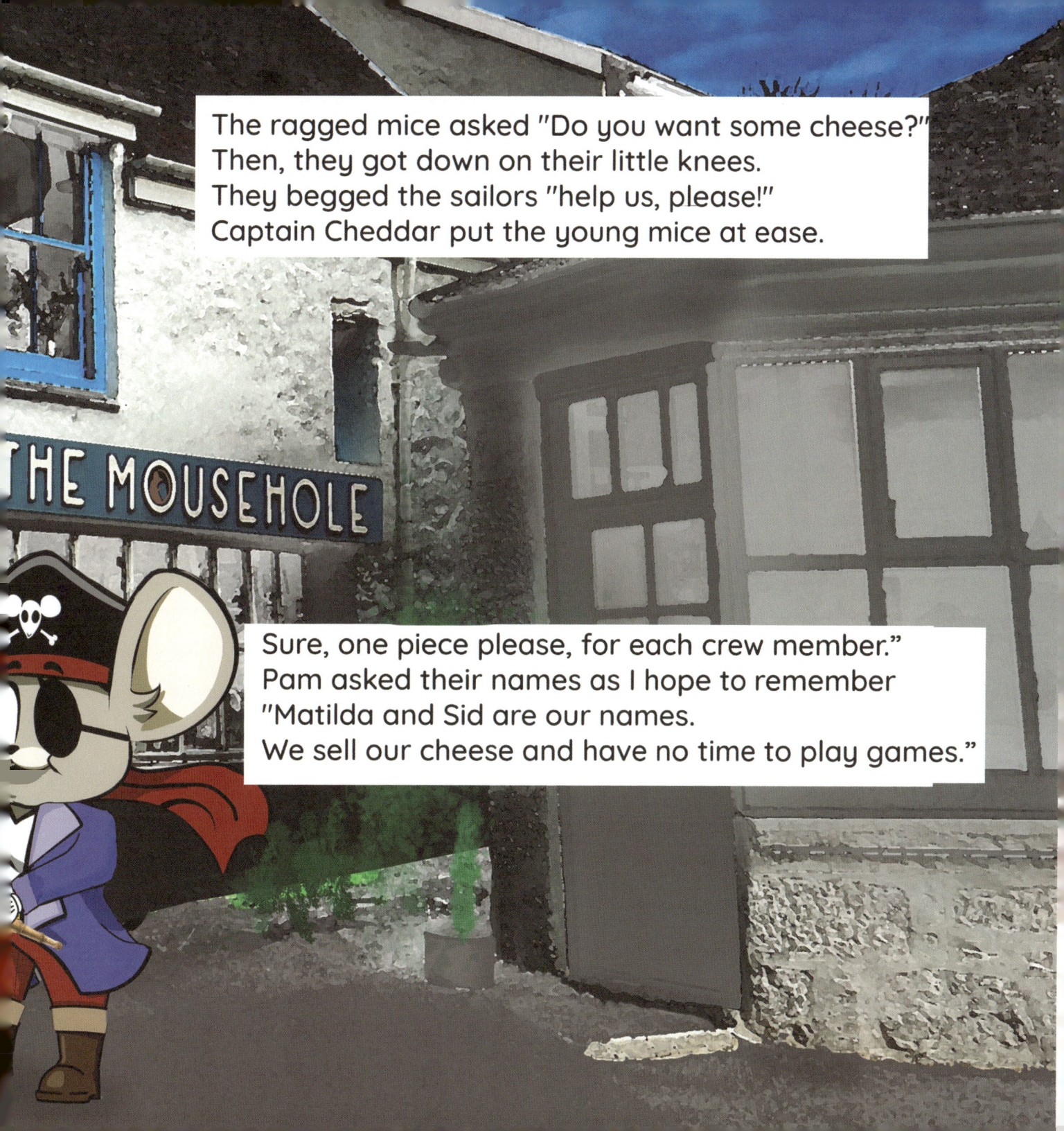

The ragged mice asked "Do you want some cheese?"
Then, they got down on their little knees.
They begged the sailors "help us, please!"
Captain Cheddar put the young mice at ease.

Sure, one piece please, for each crew member."
Pam asked their names as I hope to remember
"Matilda and Sid are our names.
We sell our cheese and have no time to play games."

"We live in the house on the top of the hill,
And our parents both work at the old mill."
Selling cheese may look funny,
We try very hard but do not earn enough money."

Matilda gave Captain Cheddar a big smile.
It's the happiest smile she had seen in a while.
Matilda asked "Do you have time to meet my mice?"
Pam Ezan said." That would be very nice."

The happy little mice lead the way up.
It was tiring, but no one gave up.
To the little house they all arrived.
The little mice let the Captain and Pam inside.

"Mama, we're home! We brought friends as a surprise."
Mama stopped in her tracks, stunned by the guys.
"My apologies-I wasn't expecting guests.
Kids clean up and put on your best."

The kids slowly came out and stood in a line.
All 23 were presented in no time.
"Why are all the children dressed in old cloth?
They look like they have been eaten by a big moth.

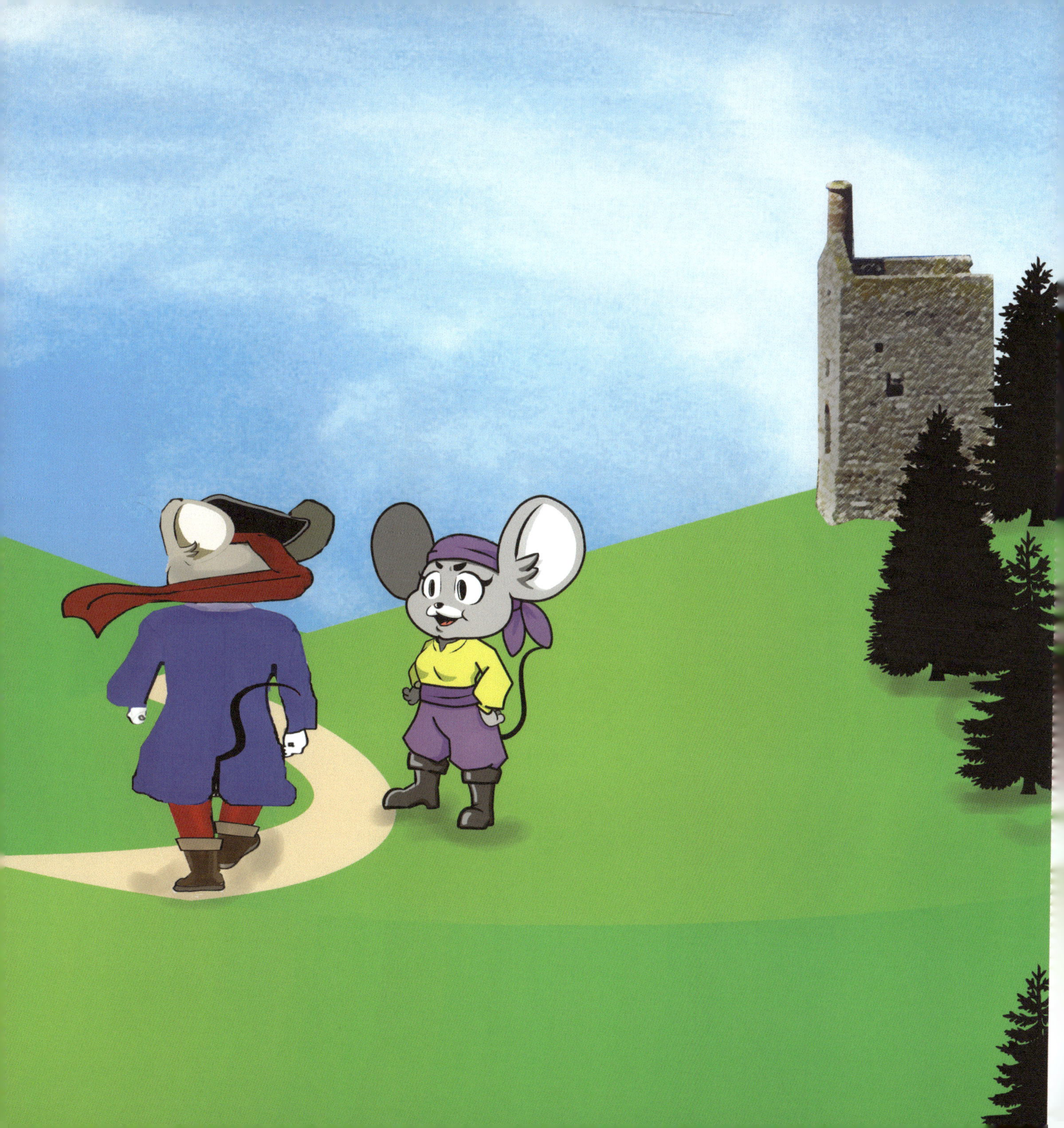

Cheddar didn't want to sound so mean.
She was just trying to understand everything.
"It is too much money for food and clothes.
We have full bellies but no socks on our toes."

Matilda explained to old Captain Cheddar.
Then she replied, "We can make this better."
Sid looked up at Pam Ezan.
He said "well, look here. I have a plan!

One day I will build a big ship just like yours.
I'll sail away to Dragon Island's shores.
I'll get treasure from the Dragon, who lives there.
Then my family will have money to spare!

"Here is where the Dragon lives on this map."
Captain said," let's do it! I know where it's at!"
Matilda and Sid asked mama for permission.
So that they are allowed to go on the mission.

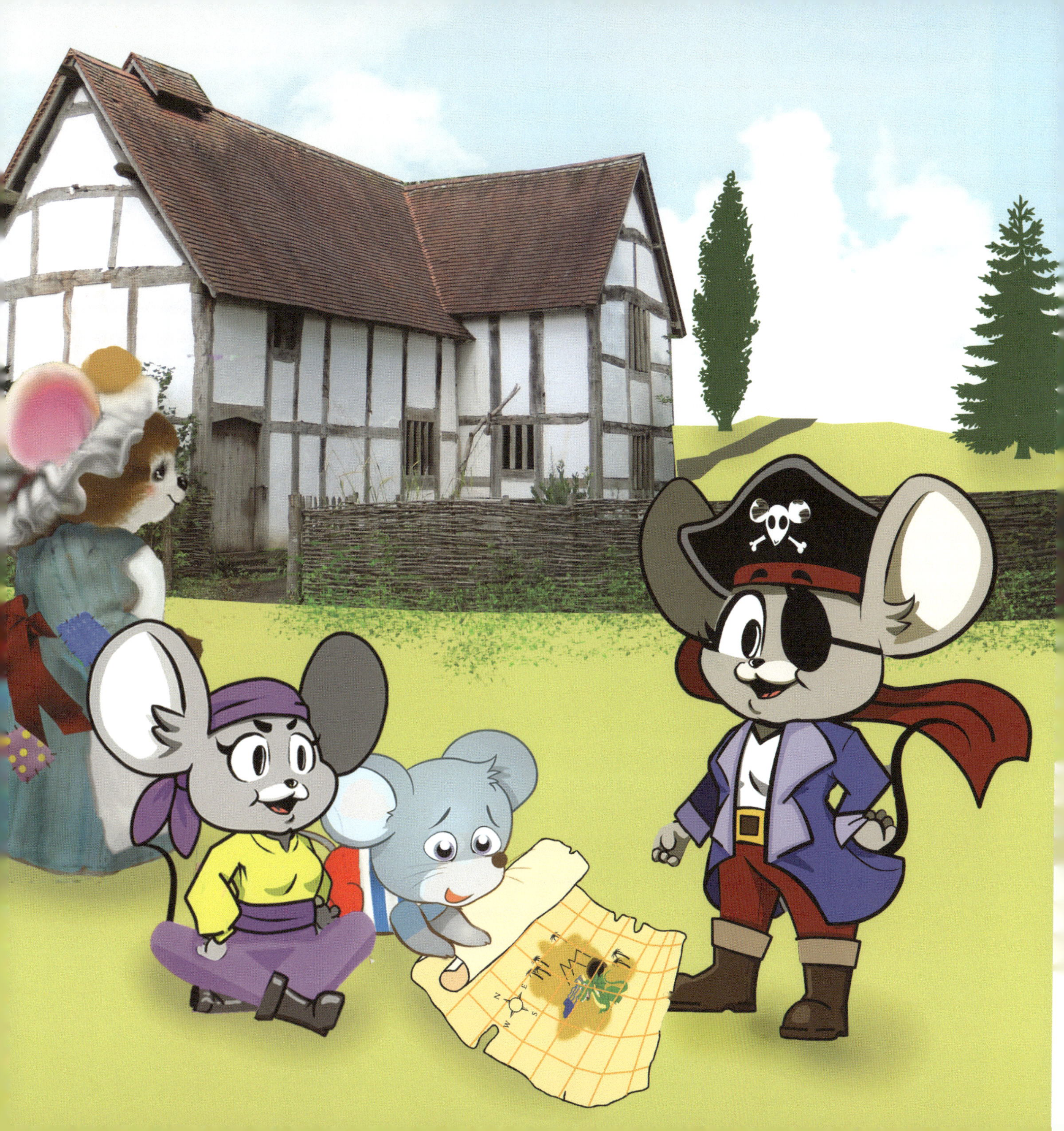

All the little mice smiled as they sailed away.
The little mice were nervous, but they were okay.
Captain Cheddar and Pam held onto them tight.
"Don't worry young mice. It will be alright."

When Captain Cheddar explained it to the crew
Out stumbled a sudden question or two.
Wensley Dale leaned to Gordon Zola's ear.
"Did they just say a Dragon? That's my biggest fear!"

"They did say a dragon!" Gordon Zola replied.
"He may be friendly! You might be surprised!"
Wensley Dale yelled "Face a dragon? Please don't let me.
He ran to his room to hug on his teddy.

He will turn us into toast, with his fire breath, at best.
"Stop it!" Said Captain Cheddar, " Go and get some rest.
Wensley could not, he had too much at stake.
He was about to face a dragon, for goodness sake.

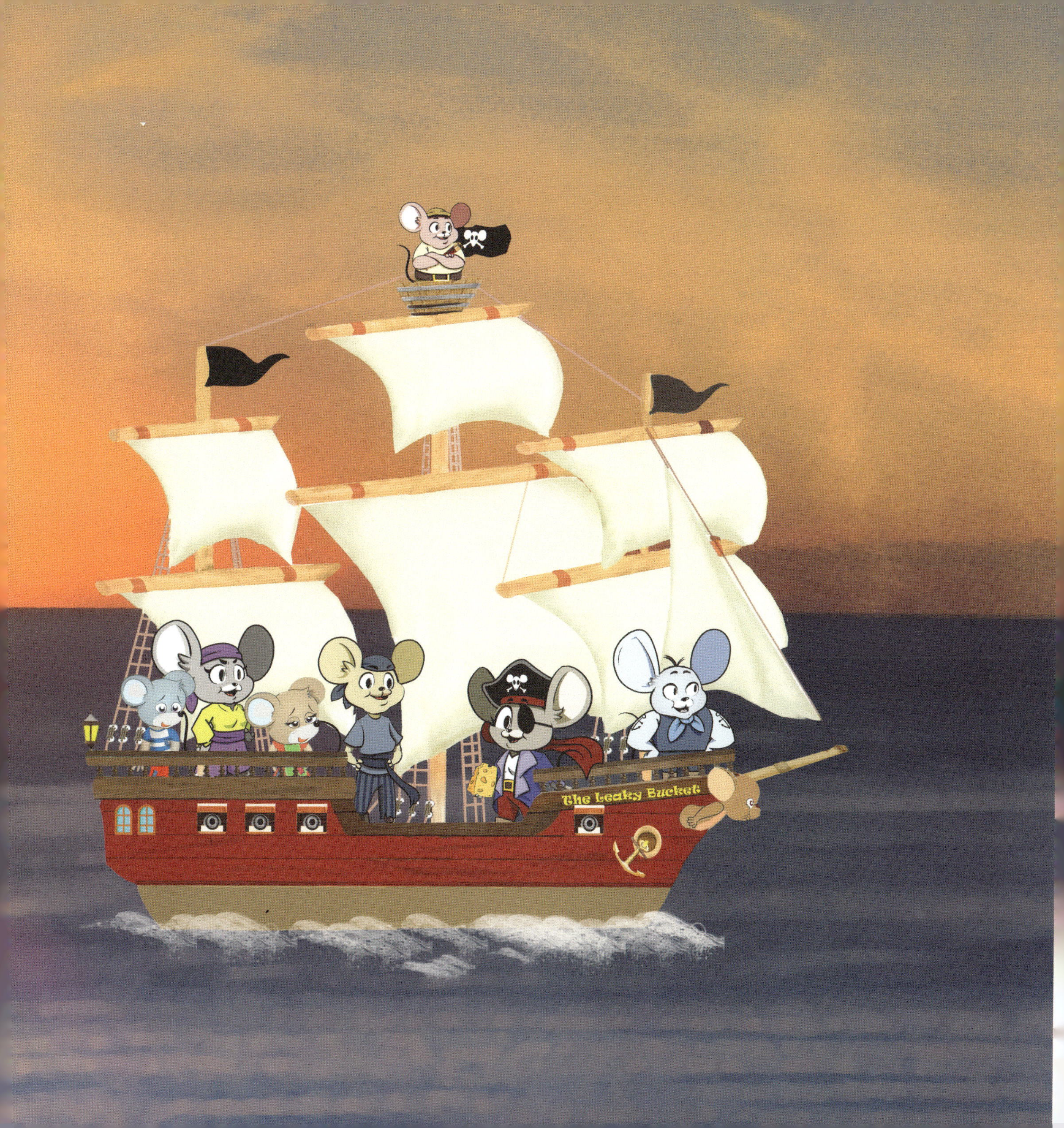
The Leaky Bucket

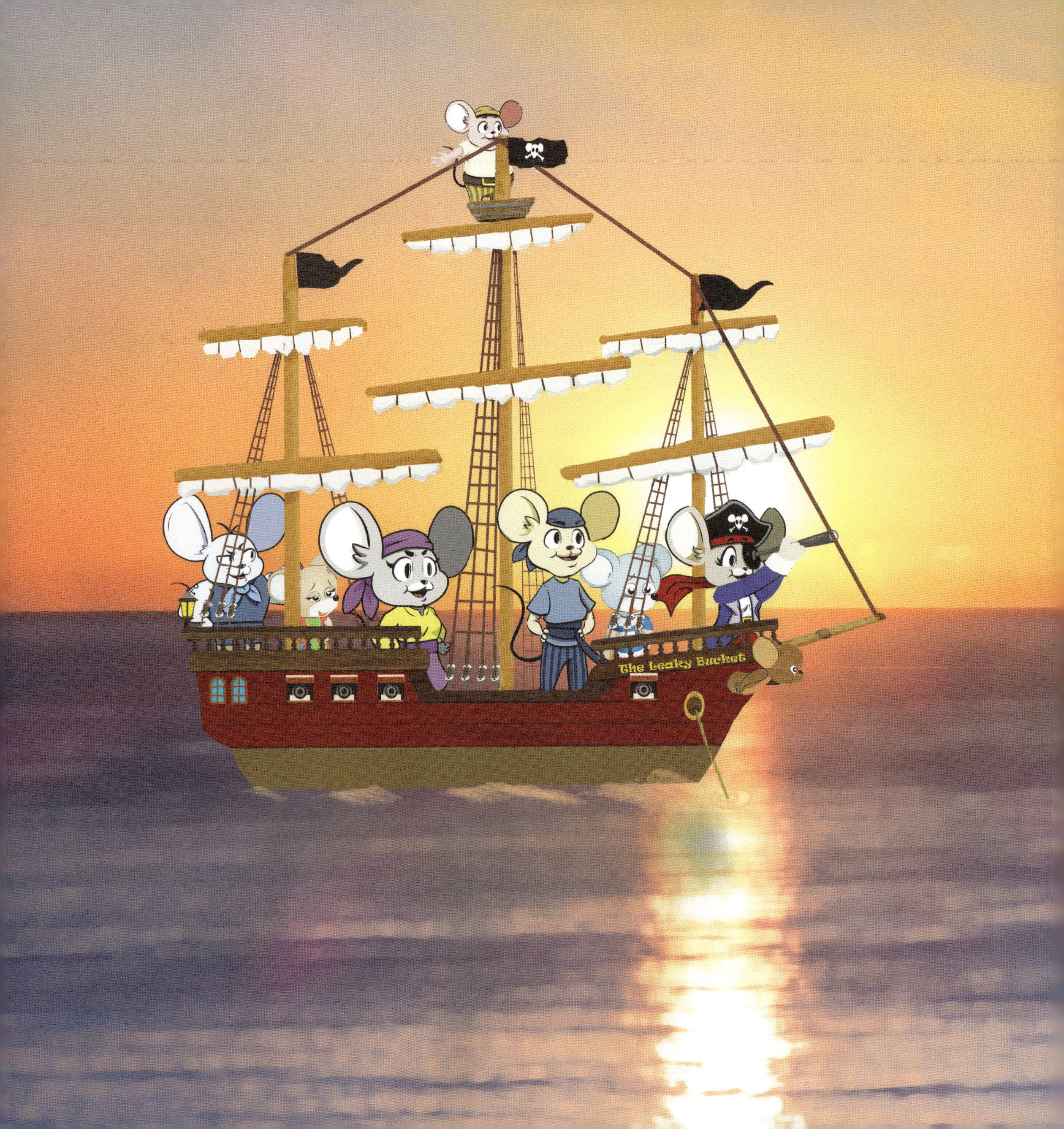
The Leaky Bucket

They anchored until the sun rose bright.
Captain Cheddar said "I've got the dragon in sight!"
The dragon had spotted the big old ship.
He was heading towards The Leaky Bucket and quick!

"Jumping jellyfish! Stand by to welcome the Dragon."
Wensley said, "No way! I wish it was gone!"
He ran off quick, leaving the crew on deck.
"Wow!" Said the Captain. "Our ship is the size of his neck."

The Leaky Buc

The Green Dragon circled over the ship.
The dragon then dove to take a dip.
Into the water, he splashed so big.
The crew was soaked and so was the rig.

Then, the dragon shouted in a deep voice.
"Leave now, while you have a choice!"
Matilda said "We want to talk to you."
He replied,"Oh, little girl, as the dragon flew.

The Leaky Bucket

"You just want to steal my treasure.
But my treasure is my only pleasure."
He then blew flames at the ship.
The mice ran to one side, it nearly tipped.

Gordon Zola gathered himself from his threat,
Loudly they replied to the Dragon so upset.
"Yes we are pirate mice but we don't steal.
We just wish to make you a deal!"

Pam Ezan shouted "I know you are kind.
I look into your eyes and kindness I find!
You didn't set fire to our ship today.
You just wanted to scare us away."

He got down to her level and he said
"Everybody wants my gold-they want me dead."
The dragon looked so lonely and very sad.
For him, there was no fun to be had.

Wensley Dale had come out of his safe space.
He rose to the deck with a sad look on his face.
"We want to ask you to share your treasure.
If you do, we will come and play together!"

"Why should I share my treasure with you?"
"Because that is what a good dragon would do.
These children are 2 of 23.
They are in need. Can't you see?

They have worn clothes and no socks.
A little bit of treasure would help a lot."
The dragon stayed quiet, without a word.
Wensley talked loud so the dragon had heard.

He said "I will give them my favourite teddy bear.
They need it more, it's only fair."
Pam Ezan said "Here is my old ring.
It's not much but it's my most valuable thing."

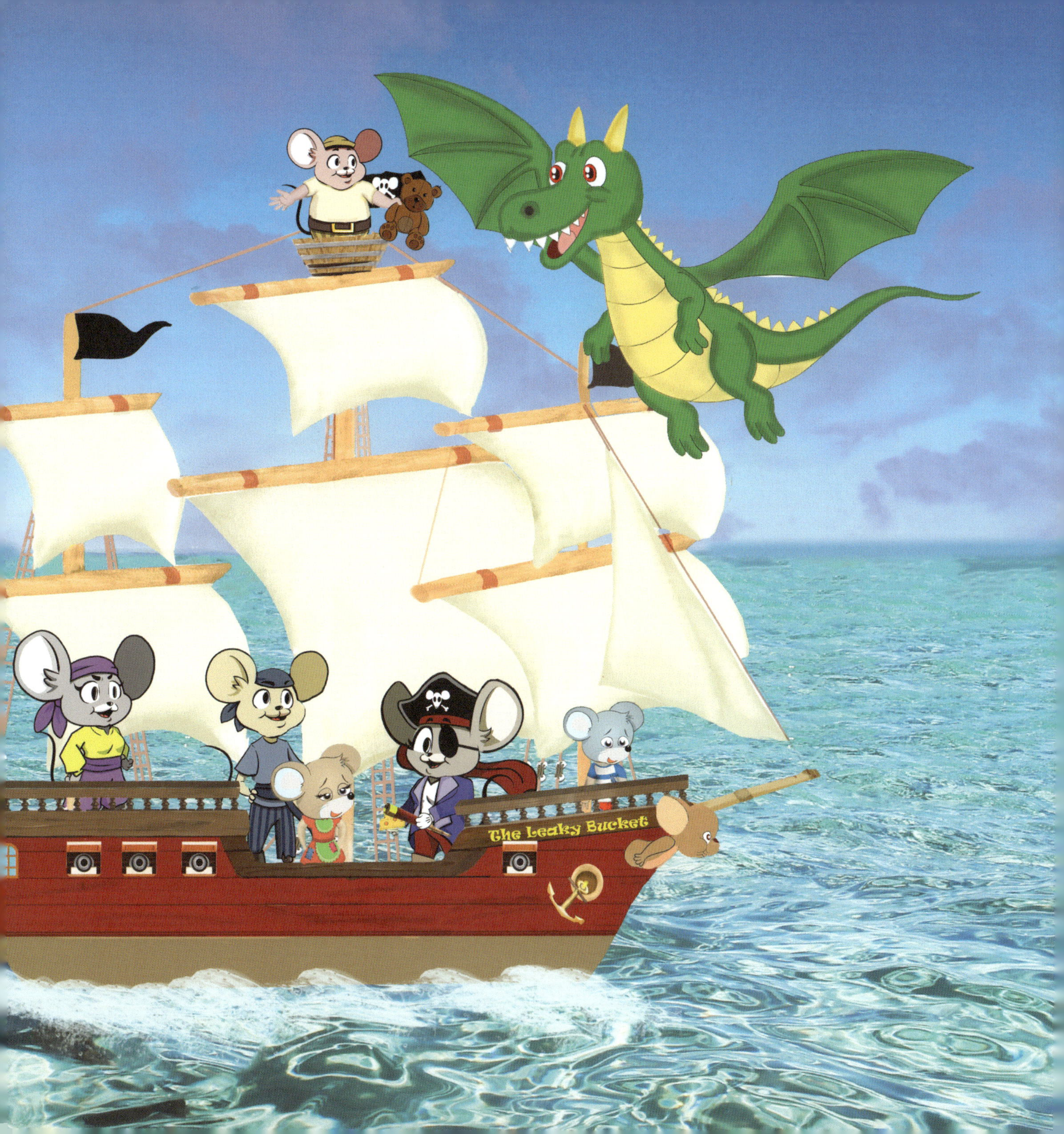
The Leaky Bucket

The Dragon wiggled his nose and drew a tear.
He began smiling from ear to ear.
"They can have some of my good old treasure,
I'd like us to be friends and play together."

He pulled them to his Wishbone Island cave.
Then he showed us all where he stayed.
Matilda and Sid couldn't believe their eyes.
There was gold and silver, in endless supplies.

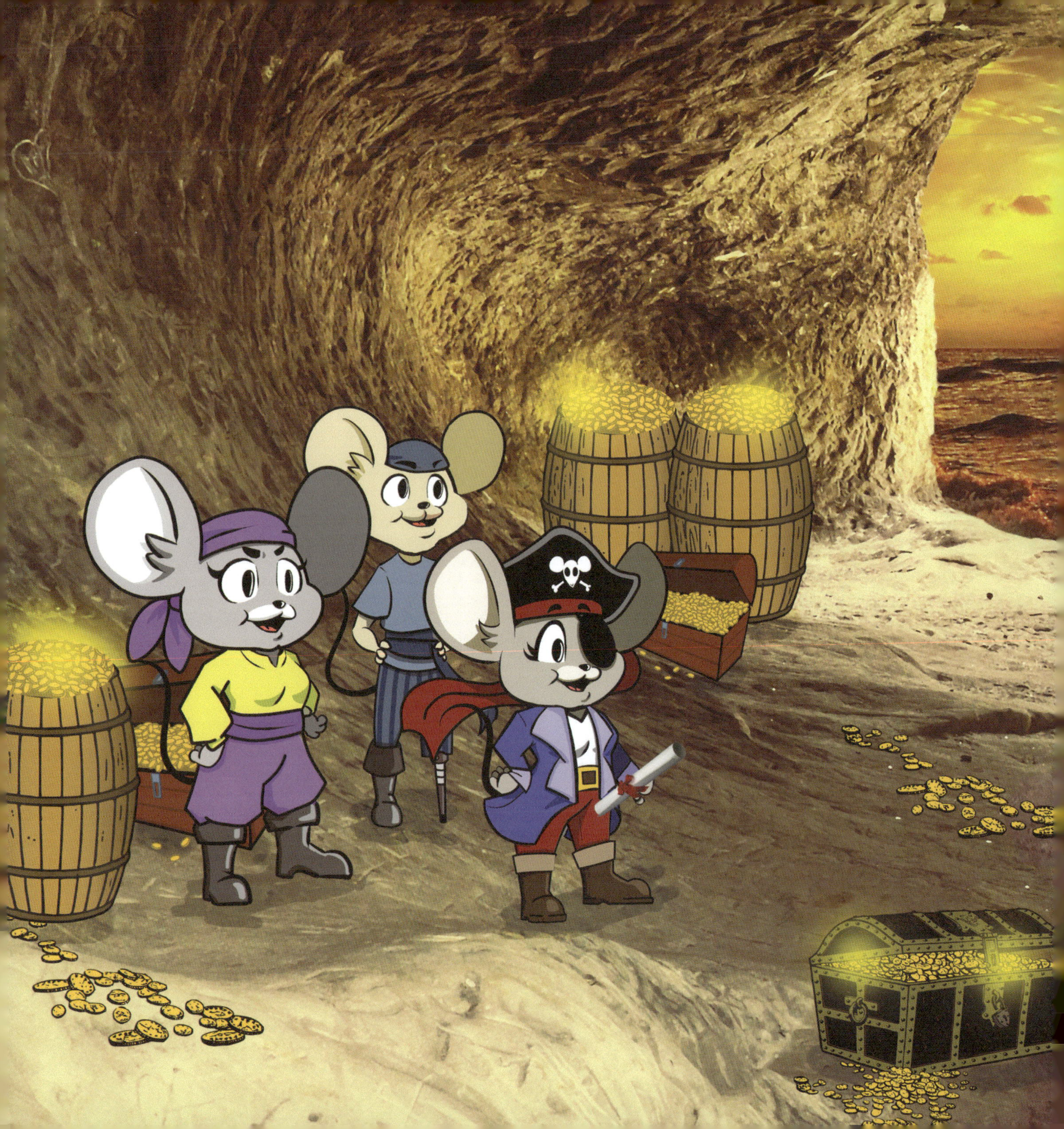

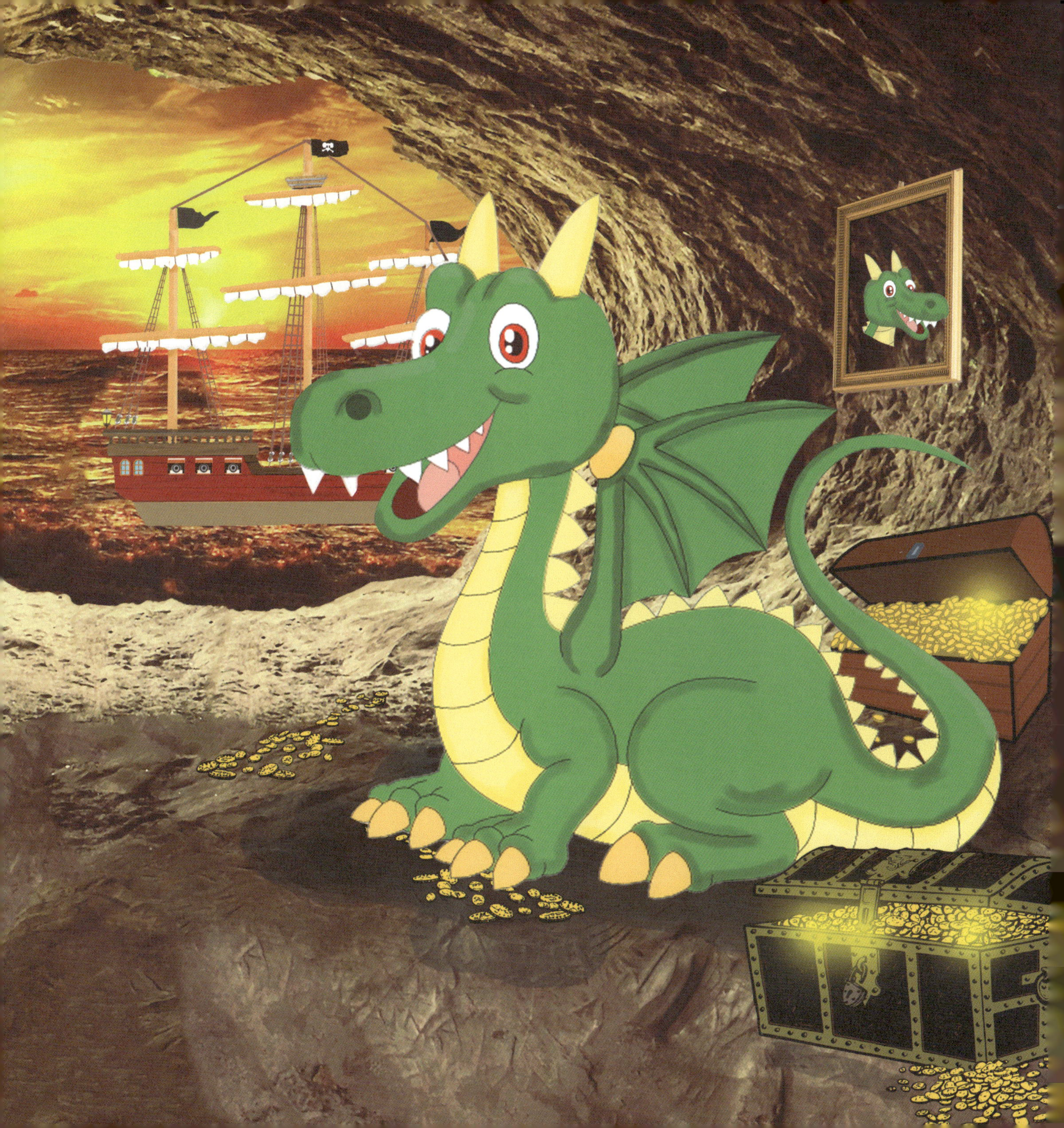

The dragon loaded the ship to the brim.
If he loaded more, the crew would have had to swim!
Matilda and Sid were so sad to leave.
They gave the dragon a chunk of cheese!

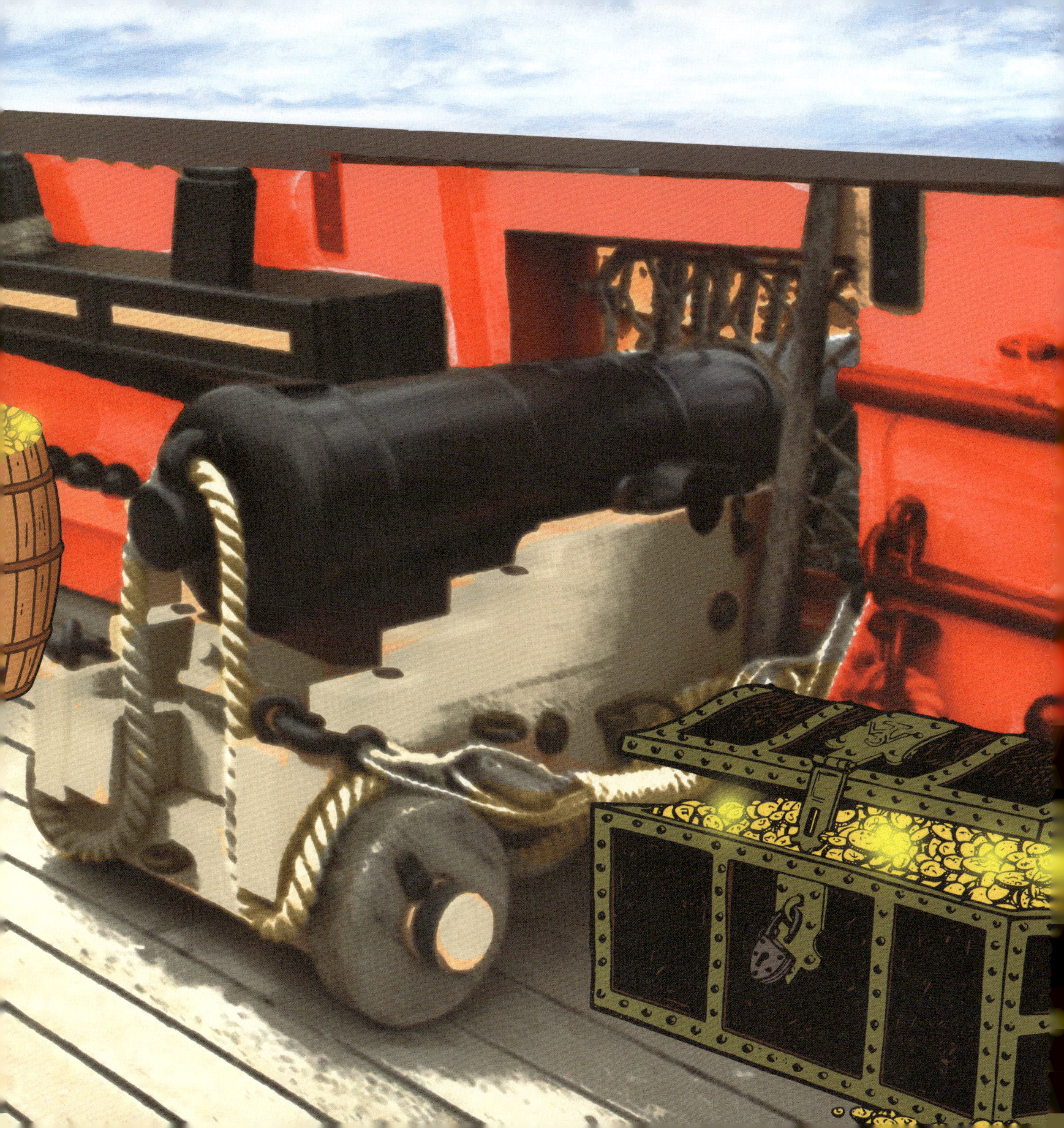

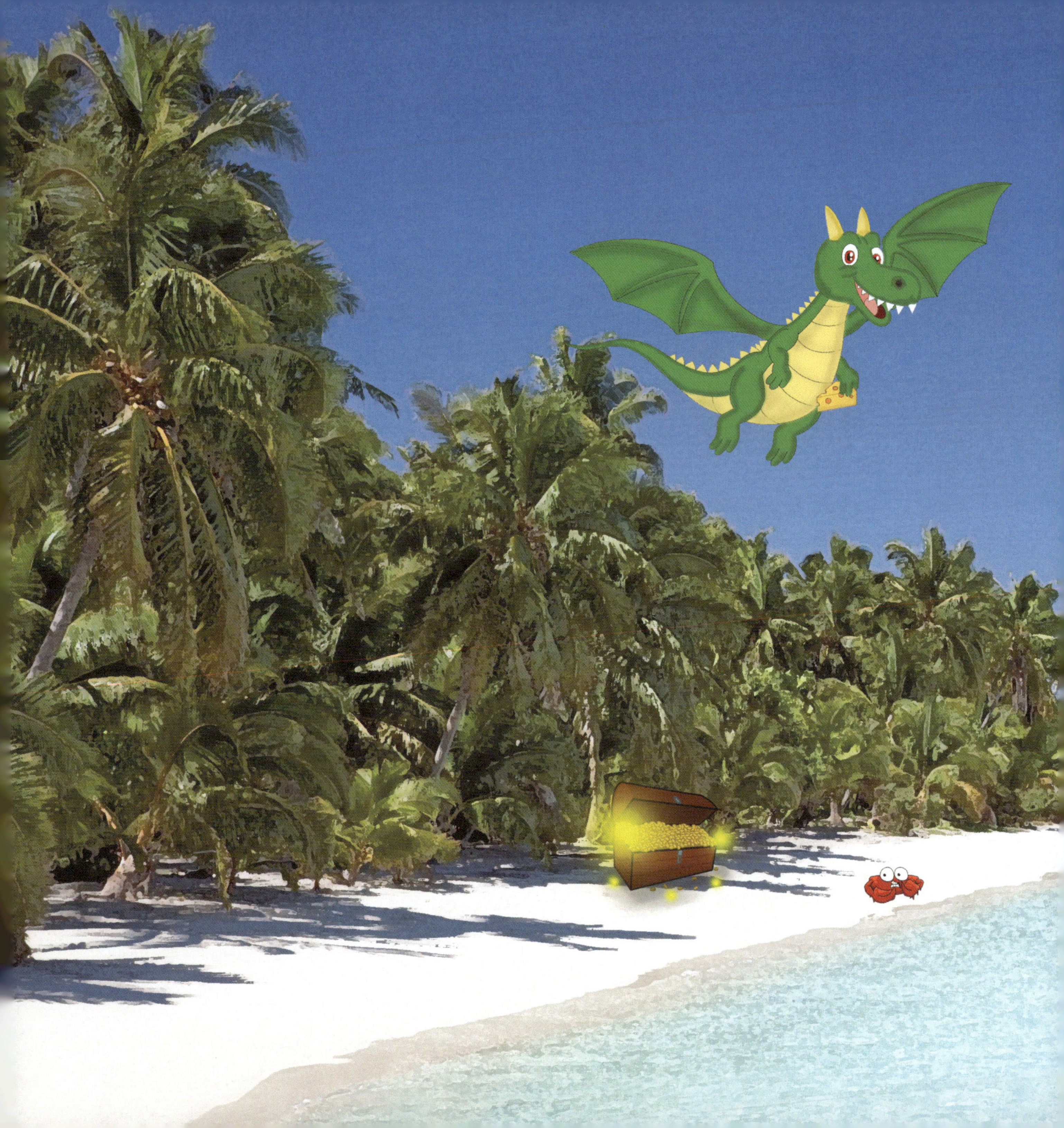

They said their good-byes and sailed away.
Little did the dragon know, they'd collect him the next day.
All 23 of those fine young mice,
All lined up along the deck, all dressed very nice.

The Little mice gathered in a big huddle
to give their friend Wyvern a loving cuddle.
You can easily see from a mile
The size of his grin and a big happy smile.

They had the carpenter make a large bucket.
They brought it to the dragon and he loved it!
They jumped inside and he took them for a ride.
Above all of Cornwall, the dragon did glide.

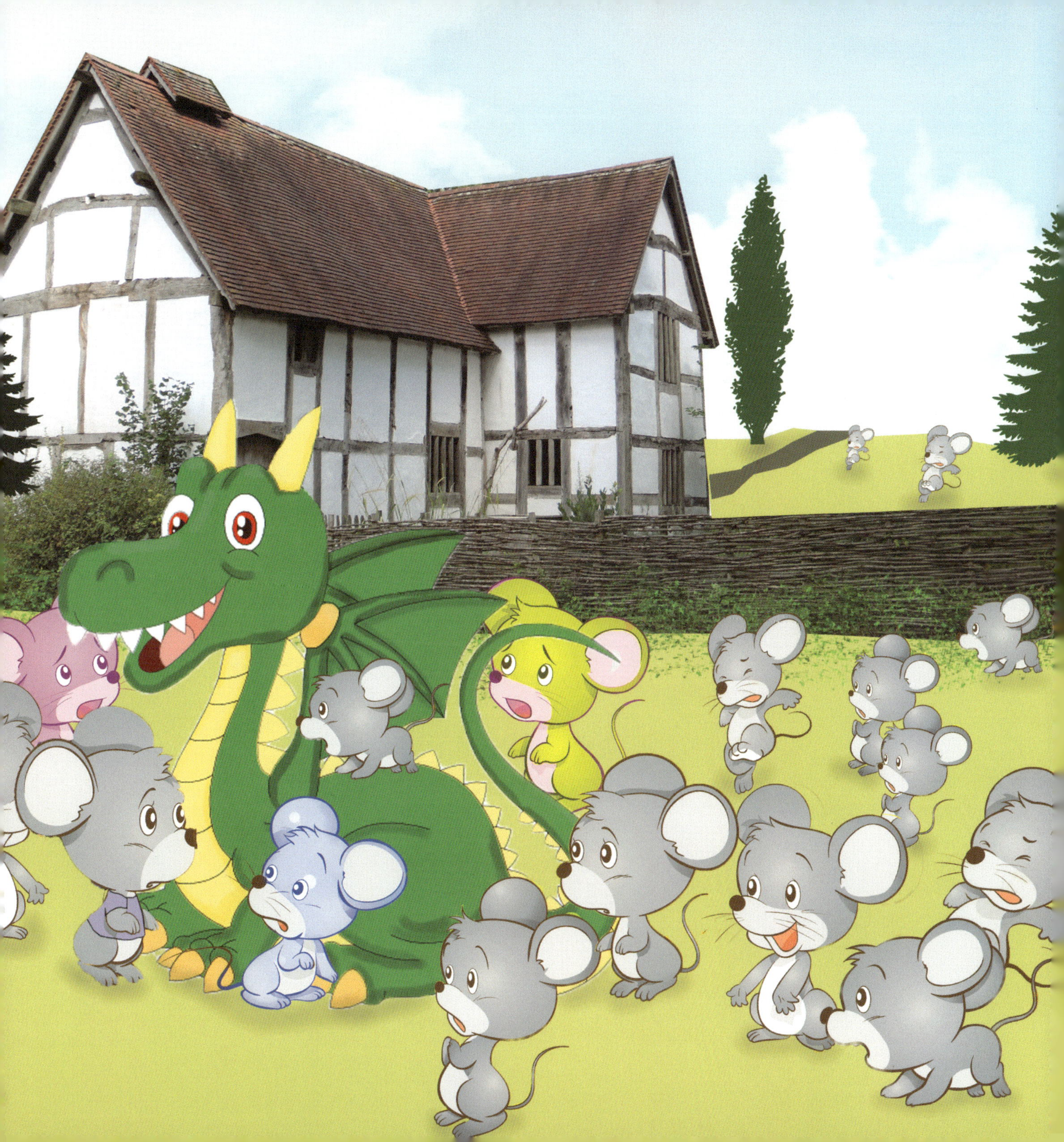

The little mice had a wonderful day.
Flying around the beach of mounts bay.
Waving and smiling up so high.
The litle mice were flying up in the sky.

How beautiful it was to finally have true friends.
Now their adventure truly never ends.
Soon the sun was going down, enough said.
Time to go home now and then off to bed.

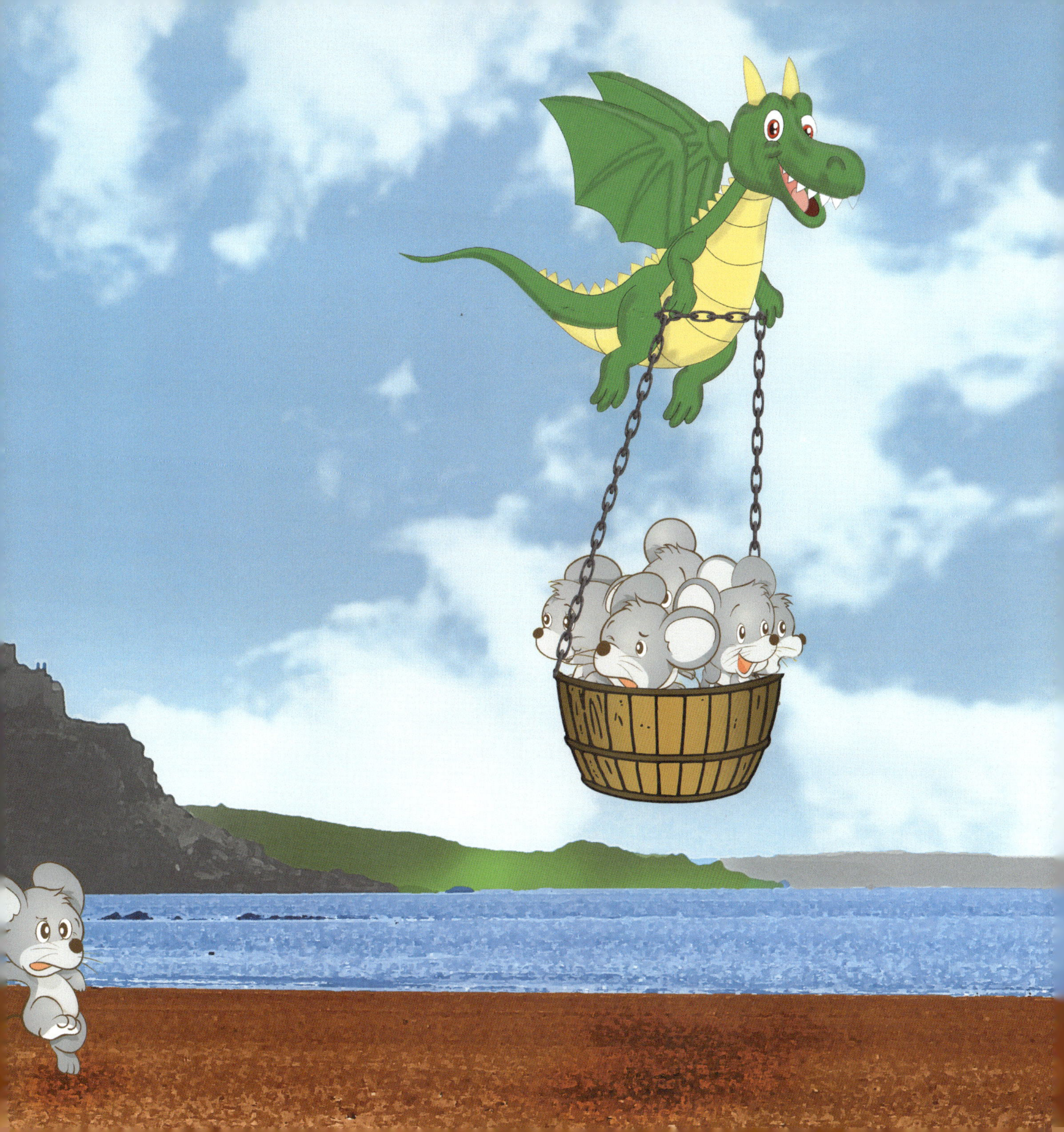

Captain Cheddar Say's

Always be kind to others
When possible, learn to share with others.
Sometimes their need is greater than yours.
See you on our next adventure.

Printed in Great Britain
by Amazon